THE GOVERNMENT
IS A PIMP

AND WE'RE LETTING THEM GET AWAY WITH IT!

AUTHOR

B. COPELAND

ATLANTA, GA

Author: Bernard Copeland
Editor: P. George

ISBN-13: 978-0-557-35396-5

Library of Congress subject heading:
Government information--United States--Miscellanea.

First Printing
Printed in The United States of America

DEDICATION

This book is dedicated to my wife Sylvia and our girls, Jaivon and Carmen, who have had to endure my rants, raves, and down right screams about government and taxes.

I've gotten it out of my system and put it down on paper. This should relieve me of the government stress and strife.

ACKNOWLEDGEMENT

Thank you, to all of you who knowingly and unknowingly participated in my crude surveys about taxes and government. Thank you for your very much valued input and candidness.

Thank you, to all of the professional tax people who enslave themselves to the understanding of the continuous and never ending, vicious cycle of tax code, tax law, tax forms, rules, and regulations. You keep the rest of us out of the reach of the Big Pimp's strangle hold. At least you try to anyway. I commend each of you that keep your battle gear ready for tackling that monster of a pet that is owned and bred by the Big Pimp; the Little Pimp. Keep reading and you'll see who is the Little Pimp. I also want to thank a very good friend of my wife, Lorraine Phillips, who recently published her first book, "How to Publish a Magazine". Lorraine is an entrepreneur and true risk taker. Thanks for the inspiration; it was right on time.

I dedicate this book to all of you that have endured or seen the lethal hand of the Big Pimps' wrath. Those of you who have tried to escape, but…let's just say that you didn't do it right, and you got caught or you simply decided to ignore the Pimp. Boy oh boy, you paid a heavy price and got PIMP SLAPPED! Oh the Big Pimp didn't slap you; but who did? The Little Pimp, his enforcer Service! This Little Pimp demanded that you open up (ante up) all of your financial books so that the Big

Pimp can see if he took enough cash from you. We'll talk more about the Pimp and his enforcer later on.

So get ready to be entertained, enlightened, and hopefully a little more interested in government and taxes. Besides, it is all about you and your hard work and the money you earn, how much of it you keep, and what you can and cannot do in this great land.

C O N T E N T S

Foreword..9

Preface..11

Political Jargon..15

Chapter 1: How Did It All Get Started?.............................17
           What is Government?...19
           Our Current Government.....................................21
           The Current Administration.................................23
           Executive Office Of The President........................25

Chapter 2: Where Did We Go wrong?..................................27
           Government Oversight..31

Chapter 3: Who is at Fault?...47

Chapter 4: How Do We escape?...53

Chapter 5: Three Little "BIG" Words..................................67
           Bureau of Internal Revenue..................................69

Chapter 6: What Are We Really Paying?............................75

Chapter 7: What If..83

Chapter 8: Still Number One...89

The End...93

Appendix..95
           The Cabinet..97
           White House Staff...99

About The Author..105

Order Form..107

8 | The Government Is A Pimp

F O R E W O R D

Wake up people and start living. Are you really free? Is this country really all that "they, the government", "they, the media", "they, the poligicians" make this country out to be? If it is so great, why are there so many problems akin to other countries that are not as great as this country? Why?

The Government Is a Pimp.

Can I be the only one that feels this way? If you honestly stopped and took a good clear look at the life and lifestyle of a politician from the state and national level you will begin to see. Do these people at this level of government really have the best interest of their constituents at the forefront of their agenda? Do they really believe that they work for the common and average citizen? Do they believe in the constitution and abide by the very laws and regulations in which the organization that governs their constituents administers? Can the politicians honestly say that they "work", and I use this term lightly, for the average working-class citizen?

P R E F A C E

Ok, let's get started. This book is basically about a machine called government that, let's say it runs and sometimes it runs really great, however it has systems and components that are broken. It has some parts in it that are outdated and are in dire need of repairs and upgrades. Yet, the big pimp will not allow the really good mechanics and technicians and a few good engineers to get in there and fix things.

Instead, we continue to allow "management" to continue "meeting" and "talking" about the problem and "how to fix it", why we should fix it and even what they think is wrong with it. Shucks, some of them even talk about real solutions and even try to implement some of the solutions on just one part of the system.

The problem with this tactic is that the government is not only a complex machine, but it is also a system with many parts and sub-systems, which can be broken in so many places. Then to add to the complexity, if you fix one thing in one area, you break something in another area…and so on and so on.

Nevertheless, regardless of how broken the machine and the system is, revenue still has the ability to flow to and through the system up to the governments' policy and rule makers.

We have all heard the phrase "oldies but goodies." This is usually said to mean that something may be old, but still operates and functions in a way that will get the job done. This phrase, however, CANNOT be applied to this government or to this system.

What If...

Looking back at history, you can see that back then, when the people got fed up with paying too much in taxes or unfair government practices, what did they do? Remember that little party they threw in Boston, around the harbor? It was a rebellion, a revolution of sorts.

What if we did something like that today? What if every law-abiding citizen, employer, entrepreneur, business, company, and organization were not to pay taxes or stop filing that dreaded tax return? What would the absolute repercussions and results be? They couldn't Pimp slap us all!!! But I'm sure they would have one hell of a time trying. How long would the government last? How long would our current way of living and surviving last? Would you do it?

What if you don't pay your state/local taxes? Some states have a "state" tax and some do not. Or at least they tell you that they don't. There are probably no state taxes collected and no law on their books anywhere, but oh boy, you had better believe they make up for it in other ways.

America is a great country. I know this, you know this and for the most part the world knows this.

But why is it great? What makes it so? What's wrong then if it's so great?

We do have "freedoms" unlike any other place in the world and all are afforded certain rights and privileges solely because we are its citizens. However, you may ask, then why would I question whether the country was great or not? Simply put, it's some of those, not all, which make up this pimp's organization, and its governing bodies that have gone awry.

The country itself and most of its people, some of its leaders, and a few of its allies are hands down some of the best people and organizations you'd ever want to know. Nevertheless, there's an evil and demonic spirit that lurks and hovers around this pimp's organization, that injects itself into some of its people, leaders, and systems through something called politics. So get ready to discover what and how this pimp came to be, what it actually is suppose to be, or not to be and do. Then start thinking about what you can do to fix it.

This book will hopefully entertain and enlighten you; and bring some thought-provoking points to the forefront and get you involved, or at least prompt you to get educated on "our" politicians (magicians) and what they're really doing with the money that they are "taking" from its citizens.

POLITICAL JARGON

Liberal   Inside Conservative   Socialist   Communist
Inside   Democrat   Republican Moderate   Liberal
Moderate   Conservative   Moderate   Outside   Dictator
The Heritage Foundation   Equal Rights   Americans for Fair
Taxation   System Organization   Rules and Regulations
        Smoke and Mirrors   By Any Means Necessary
        All Men Are Created Equal   Magician   Outside
Politician   Member   Pay to Play
Fringe Benefits   Have   Have-nots   Taxes
Taxes   Taxes   Taxes
IRS   IRS   Little Pimp   Audit
Federal Reserve   Compulsion   Income
Levy   Rule   Control   Have   Have-nots
Rich   Poor   Middle Class   Upper Class   Class by
Themselves   Wall Street
Big Pimp   Little Pimp   Enforcer
Above The Law   Break The Law   Klu Klux Klan
        Black Panthers   White Supremacy   Black Power
Peace   Human Rights   Women Rights
Animal Rights   Gay Rights   Who's Right
Who's Wrong   Left   Right   Up   Down
        We the People   America   American Citizens
        The Everyday Working Man   The Everyday Working Woman
Every Man, Woman, and Child   Constituents
You   Me   He   She   It   They   We   Us   All
The States   Enemy   Big Brother   Eye On The Target
Just a Number   Citizen   Immigrant

1

How Did It All Get Started?

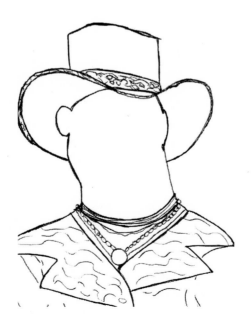

First, what is a pimp?

The word "pimp" is a slang word that is sometimes used nowadays as an insult or a compliment; it depends on which way you see it. In today's hip-hop culture and Generation X, you might hear someone say "I have a pimped-out ride" such as MTV's "Pimp My Ride," which means one's vehicle has been extremely modified and/or updated. It's now hip and cool. It can also mean going overboard with something that is being too flashy or overbearing. Something is just way too much.

The more common meaning of the word "pimp" is a male owner of a brothel (whorehouse) or someone who procures, let's say, people, for let's say clients, and takes a cut of his people's pay. Basically a pimp finds and manages clients for his brothel in order to profit from the earnings that the people make.

Typically, a pimp will not force his people to stay with him. He may offer his people protection and "benefits." His people can also work in just about any area under his control. While the pimp is living high on the hog and calling all of the shots, his people drudgingly continue working to please the Big Pimp and try to avoid his wrath.

Now as you read this book, keep this definition in mind as we look at how the government operates like a pimp. You will have an occasion to see where the government is probably even a little worse than the pimp.

The government really does no physical work. They are never in harm's way. Yet, their "people" are the ones that work and generate "income" for the government. The government gets its "cut" from its people paying up front, even before the people see it. The people are then forced to live on what's left. Then, when they do spend what's left, the government, at other levels, takes yet another cut of the people's money.

Its people are the ones that actually fight the wars that "they" wage. Its people are the ones that go hungry, homeless, and uneducated.

Let's take a look at this pimp called government and its organization.

Before we get too far into how it operates and what makes it a pimp, we need to see a little history in order to understand how it got to where it is today. Please bear with me while we get through this brief history and background lesson.

What is Government?

Taken from Webster's dictionary, you will find below the definitions of some familiar terms used with regard to government.

Government – control, rule; system of ruling; those who rule

Rule – a set guide for conduct; custom; government/govern

Tax – compulsory payment to a government; burden, strain; levy or make pay; accuse/charge

Income – money one gets as wages, salary, rent, etc

Compulsion – a forcing or being forced

Politics – science of government; political affairs, methods, opinions, scheming

Government is the body within any organization that has the authority to make and enforce laws, regulations, or rules. Typically, the term government refers to a civil government – local, provincial, or national – but commercial, academic, religious, or other formal organizations are also administered by governing bodies. Such bodies may be called boards of directors, managers, or governors or they may be known as the administration (as in schools) or councils of elders (as in churches). As long as they make and enforce rules, they are governments.

Detail from Elihu Vedder, Government (1896). Library of Congress Thomas Jefferson Building, Washington, D.C.

Government

- The body with the power to make and/or enforce laws for a country, land area, people, or organization.

- A group of people who hold a monopoly on the legitimate use of force in a given territory.

- The management or control of a system.

This is the Preamble to the Constitution.

We the people of the United States, in order to form a more perfect union, establish justice, insure domestic tranquility, provide for the common defense, promote the general welfare, and secure the blessing of liberty to ourselves and our posterity, do ordain and establish the Constitution of the United States of America.

The Constitution of the United States of America is the supreme law of the United States. It provides the framework for the organization of the United States Federal Government. This document defines the three main branches of the government and the roles and responsibilities of each. These three branches include the Congress, which is *the legislative branch*, *the executive branch* led by the President, and *the judicial branch* headed by the Supreme Court. The Constitution provides for the organization of these three branches, and it carefully and clearly outlines which powers each branch can exercise. It also reserves numerous rights for the individual states, thereby establishing the United States federal system of government.

Our Current Government

The United States of America

The Executive Branch

The power of the Executive Branch is vested in the President of the United States, who also acts as the head of state and the Commander-in-Chief of the armed forces. The President is responsible for implementing and enforcing the laws written by Congress and, to that end, appoints the heads of the federal agencies, including the Cabinet. The Vice President is also part of the Executive Branch, ready to assume the Presidency should the need arise.

The Cabinet and independent federal agencies are responsible for the day-to-day enforcement and administration of federal laws. These departments and agencies have missions and responsibilities as widely divergent as those of the Department of Defense and the Environmental Protection Agency, the Social Security Administration and the Securities and Exchange Commission.

Including members of the armed forces, the Executive Branch employs more than 4 million Americans.

The Legislative Branch

Established by Article I of the Constitution, the Legislative Branch consists of the House of Representatives and the Senate, which together form the United States Congress. The Constitution grants Congress the sole authority to enact legislation and declare war, the right to confirm or reject many Presidential appointments, and substantial investigative powers.

The Judicial Branch

Whereas the Executive and Legislative branches are elected by the people, members of the Judicial Branch are appointed by the President and confirmed by the Senate.

Article III of the Constitution, which establishes the Judicial Branch, leaves Congress significant discretion to determine the shape and structure of the federal judiciary. Even the number of Supreme Court Justices is left to Congress — at times there have been as few as six, while the current number (nine, with one Chief Justice and eight Associate Justices) has only been in place since 1869. The Constitution also grants Congress the power to establish courts inferior to the

Supreme Court, and to that end Congress has established the United States district courts, which try most federal cases, and 13 United States courts of appeals, which review appealed district court cases.

Federal judges can only be removed through impeachment by the House of Representatives and conviction in the Senate. Judges and justices serve no fixed term — they serve until their death, retirement, or conviction by the Senate. By design, this insulates them from the temporary passions of the public, and allows them to apply the law with only justice in mind, and without any electoral or political concerns.

The Current Administration

From left to right:
Back row: *Secretary of Transportation Ray LaHood, Administrator of the Environmental Protection Agency Lisa P. Jackson, Secretary of Commerce Gary Locke, Secretary of Labor Hilda Solis, United States President Barack Obama, United States Vice President Joe*

Biden, Secretary of Interior Ken Salazar, Secretary of Housing and Urban Development Shaun Donovan, Director of the Office of Management and Budget Peter R. Orszag, Chair of the Council of Economic Advisers Christina Romer, Secretary of Education Arne Duncan.

Second row: *Secretary of Agriculture Tom Vilsack, Secretary of Energy Steven Chu, Secretary of the Department of Homeland Security Janet Napolitano, Chief of Staff Rahm Emanuel, Secretary of Health and Human Services Kathleen Sebelius, United States Trade Representative Ron Kirk, United States Permanent Representative to the United Nations Ambassador Susan Rice, Secretary of Veteran Affairs Eric Shinseki.*

Third row, sitting: *Secretary of Defense Robert Gates, Secretary of Treasury Timothy F. Geithner, Secretary of State Hillary Rodham Clinton, Attorney General of the United States Eric Holder.*

The Executive Branch

President Barack & First Lady Michelle Obama

As I began writing this book and doing my research, we were in the midst of a change in administration and leadership. America was experiencing history as the first black man was elected as President of the United States of America. The United States has once again proven itself as a true world leader not just because of this fact, but because of the smooth and elegant transition of power from one administration to another. This is one of those things that make America great.

Vice President Joe & Dr. Jill Biden

Executive Office Of The President

Every day, the President of the United States is faced with scores of decisions, each with important consequences for America's future. To provide the President with the support that he or she needs to govern effectively, the Executive Office of the President (EOP) was created in 1939 by President Franklin D. Roosevelt. The EOP has responsibility for tasks ranging from communicating the President's message to the American people to promoting our trade interests abroad.

Overseen by the White House Chief of Staff, the EOP has traditionally been home to many of the President's closest advisors.

The Constitution of the United States created a bicameral (two legislative branches) Congress with both having accountability to each other. These two branches of government were intended for different audiences. One was intended to be a "people's house" that would be sensitive to public opinion. The other house was intended to represent the states. The senators in this house are to be of a more deliberate forum of 'elite wisdom' where six-year terms insulated the senators from public opinion. The Constitution ensures that the approval of both chambers is necessary for the passage of legislation.

The Senate of the United States was formed on the example of the ancient Roman Senate. The name derives from the word 'senatus', Latin for council of elders (from 'senex' meaning 'old man' in Latin). No need to expatiate on that.

So, with this bit of history, we can now see where we have been and how we got to where we are today. Government is complex yet straight-forward. It is necessary although at times it gets in the way. It is not doing enough; however, we sometimes feel that it does too much. Government has done and is doing many great things; but we also realize that it has done and still does its share of devilish deeds. With all of this, we the people still need this body with its power to make and enforce the laws and rules that will provide, protect, and secure our free liberties in this great land.

2

Where Did We Go Wrong?

The Constitution consists of a preamble, seven original articles, twenty-seven amendments, and a paragraph certifying its enactment by the constitutional convention.

This is the Preamble of the US Constitution:

"We the people of the United States, in order to form a more perfect union, establish justice, ensure domestic tranquility, provide for the common defense, promote the general welfare, and secure the blessings of liberty to ourselves and our posterity, do ordain and establish this Constitution for the United States of America."

Article One establishes legislative power and describes the Congress, which is the legislative branch of the federal government. The Congress is a bicameral body consisting of two co-equal houses: the House of Representatives and the Senate.

Article Two establishes executive power, the president, with several sections that define the qualifications, successions, pay, and appointment powers of the president, as well as the president's relations to Congress.

Article Three deals with Judicial power, which sets up the court system, the judicial branch, including the Supreme Court.

Article Four relates to states' powers and the limits between the states and the federal government.

Article Five is about amendments and how an amendment can be ratified.

Article Six on Federal power, establishes the Constitution, and the laws and treaties of the United States made according to it, to be the supreme law of the land.

Article Seven is concerned with ratification, which sets forth the requirements for the ratification of the Constitution.

So, in the case of a great country that has an organization that has a great responsibility for its people, how could it get so out of control and off track, deviating from its underlying purpose and direction? What happened? Where did we go wrong with our governing body? Where did we lose our way, failing to uphold the supreme law of the land?

Perhaps it started with the first amendment to the constitution. Or maybe it began with the second amendment, or the third, or fourth, maybe the Fifth Amendment; you get the point. Maybe we went wrong while trying to improve things for us all and make our country stronger.

In any writing, you can never really get it exactly right on the first attempt. There are always changes and improvements that can make things better. So we understand the need for these amendments.

There are currently 27 standing amendments to the Constitution.

With these last few amendments, the US Constitution still stands as the supreme law of the land, which is still the land of the "free" and the "home" of the brave. So, is it finished? Is it complete? Does it hold the values, the rights, the direction which the forefathers initially intended?

I want each of you to read the US Constitution and do your best to understand it and commit it to memory. And keep the meaning and purpose of the constitution in mind the next time you go to vote on any item on any ballot.

So with that in mind, here are the Amendments included in the US Constitution.

The current amendments to the U.S. Constitution:
www.usconstitution.net/const.html

Amendment 1 - Freedom of Religion, Press, Expression
Amendment 2 - Right to Bear Arms
Amendment 3 - Quartering of Soldiers
Amendment 4 - Search and Seizure
Amendment 5 - Trial and Punishment, Compensation for Takings
Amendment 6 - Right to Speedy Trial, Confrontation of Witnesses
Amendment 7 - Trial by Jury in Civil Cases
Amendment 8 - Cruel and Unusual Punishment
Amendment 9 - Construction of Constitution
Amendment 10 - Powers of the States and People

The first ten amendments to the U.S. Constitution are considered *the Bill of Rights*. The Bill of Rights keeps Congress from making any laws targeting an establishment of religion or prohibiting the free exercise thereof; it forbids the infringement of the right of people to keep and bear arms; and prohibits the federal government from depriving any person of life, liberty, or property without due process of law.

Amendment 11 - Judicial Limits
Amendment 12 - Choosing the President, Vice President
Amendment 13 - Slavery Abolished
Amendment 14 - Citizenship Rights
Amendment 15 - Race No Bar to Vote
Amendment 16 - Status of Income Tax Clarified
Amendment 17 - Senators Elected by Popular Vote
Amendment 18 - Liquor Abolished
Amendment 19 - Women's Suffrage
Amendment 20 - Presidential, Congressional Terms
Amendment 21 - Amendment 18 Repealed
Amendment 22 - Presidential Term Limits

Amendment 23 - Presidential Vote for District of Columbia
Amendment 24 - Poll Taxes Barred
Amendment 25 - Presidential Disability and Succession
Amendment 26 - Voting Age Set to 18 Years
Amendment 27 - Limiting Congressional Pay Increases

Now as you can see, the Bill of Rights appears to limit governmental powers and provide citizens with specific rights. Therefore, I say read it, learn it, and let's hold the elected officials to it.

As I asked earlier, where did we go wrong? Maybe we started to go wrong with this part of the governmental organization, the GAO. Perhaps we should fire everyone in this department. What's the GAO, you might ask?

Government Oversight

Overseeing of the executive branch is an important Congressional check on the President's power and a balance against his discretion in implementing laws and making regulations.

The main way the Congress conducts the supervision is through hearings. The House Committee on Oversight and Government Reform and the Senate Committee on Homeland Security and Government Affairs are both devoted to overseeing and reforming government operations, and each committee conducts the overseeing in its policy area.

Congress also maintains an investigative organization, the Government Accountability Office (GAO). Founded in 1921 as the General Accounting Office, its original mission was to audit the budgets and financial statements sent to Congress by the Secretary of the Treasury and the Director of the Office of Management and Budget. Today, the

GAO audits and generates reports on every aspect of the government, ensuring that taxpayers' dollars are spent with the effectiveness and efficiency that the American people deserve.

The executive branch also polices itself: there are sixty-four Inspector Generals, each being responsible for a different agency, and each regularly auditing and reporting on the agencies to which they are attached.

Government is established for a wide range of reasons. However, it is established primarily to control greed and oppression, maintain order, protect natural rights, and to ensure the social well-being of its people.

With that being said, it seems as if ALL of these political pimps currently in government have completely forgotten about this little stem of government, the GAO, which is designed to oversee all of the spending and the unscrupulous laws that are detrimental to the interests of those that are being governed. Why? I feel that there is no accountability whatsoever in what the government is doing with the American Taxpayers' money. No one in government appears to have the American People and their liberties in sight. (Keep in mind that this is just my humble opinion.)

For example, have you heard of this program?

Hope for Homeowners

This program sounds great at the outset but one must read all the details to know exactly who benefits from this program.

The Bush Administration introduced the "Hope for Homeowners" program in 2008 in an effort to "help" more struggling families keep their homes. This program was designed as a mortgage assistance program for homeowners facing risk of foreclosure. The program will refinance mortgages for those having difficulties making their payments, but can't afford a new mortgage that would be insured by the other government entities such as HUD and FHA.

The program is only available to owner occupants and will offer 30-year fixed rate mortgages. Banks will have to lower the existing mortgage to 90 percent of the new appraised value of the property.

Borrowers must be eligible and work with their lender to get the benefits:
- The home is their primary residence, and they have no ownership interest in any other residential property, such as second homes.
- Their existing mortgage was initiated on or before January 1, 2008, and they have made at least six payments.
- They are not able to pay their existing mortgage without help.
- As of March 2008, their total monthly mortgage payments due were more than 31 percent of their gross monthly income.
- They certify that they have not been convicted of fraud in the past 10 years, intentionally defaulted on debts, and did not knowingly or willingly provide material false information to obtain their existing mortgage(s).

Sounds good, right? However, this program has one little catch that I found interesting.

- The borrower must agree to share with FHA both the equity created at the beginning of this new mortgage and any future appreciation in the value of the home.

Yet another interesting thing in the program is that if the home is sold or refinanced, the homeowner will share the equity with FHA ranging from a 100 percent FHA share after the first year to a minimum of 50 percent after five years.

I guess if you're truly desperate and don't plan on selling your home very soon, this may not be such a bad idea. But you must read all the details to be fully aware of the consequences.

Just remember that once you sign on to this program, if and when you sell your home, the government is entitled to 50% of any profit from the sale of your home. Now this little detail will not probably be clearly spelled out, so be sure to ask.

I encourage you to see if you can find out more information about this program. See what facts and information you can find to indicate that this would be a win-win program. WAKE UP, please! People, please never sign a contract or ANY legal document without first reading it completely and thoroughly. No matter how long it takes you to read it, read it. If they don't want you to read it or don't allow you to do so, then don't sign it, AND be sure to ask questions about anything you don't understand or don't like and get it changed. If enough folks do this enough times, perhaps this will force the legal and contractual document world to simplify contracts. Say What You Mean and Mean What You Say.

You can get more information about the program at: www.hud.gov/hopeforhomeowers.

This is what I mean: the government will not even sneak things in, they will blatantly put things in, tell you about it, and know with a lot of confidence that you will not do anything about it. And when I say put things in, I mean make laws, policies, rules, regulations, programs, benefits, etc., for the better or the worse, and not advertise it.

For example, a benefit that you may or may not be aware of is the **Work Investment Act of 1998 (WIA)**.

The Workforce Investment Act (WIA) basically provides job training funds for adults, dislocated workers (those that have been laid off) and youth. However, the act does not provide funds for just any type of training, but training and funds only for specific areas of need.

How do you find about this program? Well, this information "should" be provided to you when you go to the unemployment office. But do they advertise this program? In many cases, the answer is "no". There are so many people needing this financial assistance for training and I am sure the government is selective in giving out information on this program.

Another example of blatant government action is at the state level. In the state of Georgia, a vehicle emission is required to get to a state tag for your vehicle. Initially, the fee for a vehicle emission was only five dollars and it was required each year. No big deal, right? It was only five bucks. Well, someone in this state level pimp's organization decided, 'hey, I know how we can make more money on this emissions thing. Raise the fee to twenty-five dollars but only require the emission every two years. The public will gripe, but hey, IT IS REQUIRED and IT IS LAW!!! What can they do?'

So guess what, they raised the fee. How long did it last? One term! That's right, only one term. And what did "we the people" do? Oh, there was griping and moaning, but nothing was actually done. This emission fee is still twenty-five dollars, but now it's back to being required every year. That's right, they made a drastic change right in front of your face and we did absolutely nothing about it. A fee that goes from five dollars to twenty-five dollars and not a single increase in benefits or service. SAY IT AIN'T SO!!! But don't get me wrong here; I am definitely for a cleaner and healthier environment, and I do the necessary maintenance on my vehicle to ensure it doesn't pollute unnecessarily. But most new vehicles already meet strict EPA guidelines so that they don't pollute! All this makes you wonder, doesn't it? The point I'm trying to make is that we have to constantly educate ourselves and stay attuned to changes that the government makes. It's little things like this emissions fee. These things slip through the cracks unnoticed but cost the taxpayers a lot of money.

Consequently, you may be adversely affected by a policy or miss out on an opportunity to gain back some of what you have lost to the government. Now does this sound like something a pimp would do?

Big FAT Government

Government has become like a tremendously overweight person that has grown so large that he cannot even leave his own room, let alone leave the house.

How did we lose control of our government and the process of fair taxation? How did we lose the process of No Taxation without Representation? Do those in power really and truly believe that they work for the people that they govern?

Government has gotten way too big and has a reach much too far into our personal lives. I know it, you know it, and even the government knows it. And yet we still do nothing about it.

I have a task for you. Almost every elected official has an email address, public mailing address, or phone number. This includes your local public servant all the way up to the top dog, the president of the United States. Your task is simple, to email, write a letter, or call several elected officials in your line of representatives and ask this one question:

Who do you work for?

Let's see what kind of response you get.

The government currently has more to do with our personal lives than you know. AND WHY? Because we let them do it. As long as we continue to vote for, be in favor of, or lean to a specific political 'party' and <u>not</u> hold the individuals who are elected to do a job accountable, then we will never have a government that is for the people and by the people.

That's right, yeah, go ahead and sit back and whine and scream about jobs, taxes, and welfare. All of the complaining and talking in the world will not change a thing. We must first educate ourselves on what the government is <u>supposed</u> to be doing; then we need to examine what it is they <u>are</u> doing, and then <u>hold them accountable</u>. And if they're not doing the job, FIRE THEM! Yes, FIRE THEM, we have that power.

The bad part about this is that the politicians know this fact too! That is why they talk convincingly, telling you what you want to hear and then they turn around and do something completely different. Why, because they can and because we allow them to do it. We are all too busy working and 'enjoying' our so-called freedoms and personal lives, while the government is busy scamming us through its smoke and mirrors.

So many politicians have so obscured the real essence of politics and policy that even those that truly intend to uphold the constitution and do what is right for the people in what they do, have become so frustrated and, at times, compelled to succumb to the evil that has corrupted their colleagues. However, most of the good guys do not give in to the greed and evil that plague most politicians after a couple of years of political and governmental power. Instead, they continue to make honest, moral, and common sense decisions on what is best for the American people. Even though it is tough, and there is some give and take, they are sensible and think about their constituencies and about Mom and Pop and the average Joe.

There are still a few good politicians who continue to fight the good fight. This is an assumption. They continue to voice the people's voice and this, my friends, is what keeps the show going. This is why some things get done and a lot of things do not. These good politicians are outnumbered and are basically kept in place for public appearances and media pong. They are used to telling us what they think we want to hear.

For example, take one of your local elections. Do you really know exactly what it is you are voting for each and every time you go to the polls? Do you have enough information to know what the ramifications are on voting 'yes' or 'no' on this moratorium or this 'temporary sales tax', or this amendment? Can you actually get the information on and the background of what it is that this commissioner or representative wants you to vote yes or no on?

Can you honestly say that you know just what each item on the ballot is and what the effect of a yes or no vote will be? Not really, huh? Furthermore, when a local, state, or national campaign begins, you never really get an opportunity to understand the qualities or values of a candidate, because the politicians are so busy, with the help of the media, slinging personal attacks at each other and digging up dirt on what the others did in their personal lives and past political careers. They talk about one or two particular issues, and then they will "skew" the true meaning of that issue to make either himself or herself look good, or the other person look bad. It's all just smoke and mirrors.

What we want to know is what they are going to do for us, the American people; the people who will put them where they want to be. Where do you stand Mr. Politician? What can you do to help us Ms. Politician? How can you change things for my family and me? What specifically are you going to do to reduce crime? Can you tell us a specific better plan for health care? Can you explain what you really mean in a plain and simple language?

Let's get our politicians to explain to us in plain English what the house bill means. What are the pros and cons of voting either way on a particular ballot item?

Hear me good folks, I'm not talking about Democrat or Republican, Liberal or Green party. I'm talking about plain and simple laws and regulations that will affect our daily lives and our individual economic stability.

I'm trying to do my part to be the good citizen. I work, I pay my taxes, both those taxes that they TAKE from me before I even see a paycheck and those that they TAKE after I get my paycheck. Then once a year, on April 15th, I check with the Little Pimp to make sure I have paid them enough! When will it ever end?

Most of us want to succeed in life and pursue "the American dream" or just our dreams and desires. And we want to do it legally and without hurt, harm or danger to others. SHUCKS, most of us want to help others succeed too! How about you Mr. or Ms. Politician?

There is a local radio talk-show host who made a suggestion that, I believe, is at least a start to getting us all to thinking about solutions, rather than continuing to point the finger and spotlight the problem. This is what I always ask for from anyone who raises a problem or points out what is wrong with something. If you are going to bring a problem to the table, you must bring a solution along with it. Otherwise, keep it to yourself.

Anyway, this guy is very provocative and entertaining. His name is Neal Boortz. He and Congressman John Linder wrote a book about an alternative to the IRS and our current tax system. The book is on the Fair Tax. The Fair Tax is not new, it's just scary, for politicians that is. All of us know that we definitely need to do something about the current tax system. It's broken and it only affects the everyday working citizens and not anyone in state or federal government. It especially does not affect those who are the policy, rule, and lawmakers. This is the reason why they blatantly and carelessly waste and pillage the tax dollars away.

So, what did Neal say that was so interesting? He said something to this effect. We should get Congress to change the current tax laws by introducing a resolution into Congress that has three parts:
Part 1 – Constitutional convention
Part 2 – Term limits for house of representative congressmen to 6 years
Part 3 – Repeal the 16th amendment of the constitution, the IRS and
       Taxes

There was something about the 17th amendment too, but I don't recall. Something about getting rid of it too.

I say, introduce the Fair Tax. Let's at least get some dialogue going so that we may begin to do something about the current system that is horribly broken. Let us clear up some of the smoke and break a few of those mirrors.

In their book, Neal and Congressman Linder talk about what is needed to overhaul this outdated and broken down tax system. I admit, the Fair Tax may not be perfect, but anything would be much better than what is currently in place. Why not try it? Why not debate it in public and weigh all the pros and cons of it against the current tax laws and systems?

Can anyone honestly, clearly, and accurately state why the current tax system and laws are so complicated? Can anyone give the American people a clear and concise answer as to why the current tax system has laws that change every single year?

I mean, what are taxes? Why do we pay them? Why do we pay so many? I understand that governmental bodies, in order to provide services, collect taxes and give protection to the people they govern. Everyone can understand that. We even understand the pimp's "withholding" idea. We understand this idea of withholding so that we don't have to sit down and write that check once a year for all of the services and protection that the ruling authorities provide to the citizens.

What we need is to hear solutions -- real tangible solutions -- to the problems we face everyday. We do not need to hear about the problems we already know and live with. Tell us about solutions that we can implement. Tell us about real ways to fix the problems that we are facing today and will face tomorrow. Most Americans are willing to roll up their sleeves and pitch in for well-thought-out plans and solutions for fixing problems and preparing for future issues. Most Americans are willing even to pay for the implementation of good solid solutions that will work to make the lives of the people more comfortable and meaningful and less taxing.

Now we too must be willing to hear viable and relevant solutions, and then commit ourselves to doing our part in order to see them through to fruition. We all have a part to play in our own financial stability, safety, and success. Don't wait for handouts if you can contribute to making things better for yourself.

If you think that our current tax system is broken and needs to be fixed, then take action and write to your state senator, congressman/congresswoman and tell them just that. Let them know that something needs to be changed to simplify our current tax system. Whether you support the Fair Tax or not, something needs to be changed.

As I wrote and researched, I asked others about government and taxes. So I decided to do an impromptu survey, which is described below. Bear in mind that these were individuals with their own opinions who were randomly selected. No one was coerced or persuaded in any way.

Government

An Impromptu Survey

This impromptu survey was done with just about anyone who would answer this question. These are actual responses from the participants. As you can see, some responses are similar and have the same tone.

<u>Question</u>

If you could sum up all of your thoughts on TAXES in one sentence, what would you say?

The following are responses from a few tax-paying citizens.

"Taxes Sucks".

"It can be revisited – It should be revisited."

"They are a big rip off."

"They Suck."

"I look forward to the end of the year."

"They're wrong . . . there is no law . . . not seeing where the money goes."

"Everybody should pay their fair share . . . everyone should pay."

"Hire a tax accountant and let them worry about it. Here's my paper and my money."

"Income Tax was supposed to be a temporary thing, who made it permanent?"

"Crooked."

"They suck."

"Taxes are an unfair but often necessary burden that is needed to maintain the stability of a country."

"Need to be equalized and reduced."

"We need to eliminate taxes."

"We should abolish all taxes and go to just one tax."

What would your answer be?

3

Who Is At Fault?

With a little more history, here we can see how the problems continued to cause havoc on its people.

The following is from The American Republic history book.

1865   Andrew Johnson becomes president on Lincoln's assassination and carries the Great Emancipator's Reconstruction program forward.

1866   Congress, under Radical domination, adapts the 14th Amendment, as momentous a step for business regulation as for race relations.

1867   Alaska (admitted as 49th state in 1958) is purchased from Russia. The organization of the secret Patrons of Husbandry starts the farmers protest against industrialism known as the Granger Movement.

1868 The failure of the Senate by one vote to remove President Johnson after his impeachment by the House; he preserves the presidency with complete subservience to Congress.

1869 The first transcontinental railroad is completed.

1872 The Amnesty Act restoring political privileges to most citizens of the late Confederacy opens the way to the restoration of "white supremacy" in the South.

1876 The Centennial Exposition in Philadelphia highlights the economic progress of the Nation in the hundred years since the Declaration of Independence.

1876 Mark Twain publishes *The Adventures of Tom Sawyer*, to be followed eight years later by *The Adventures of Huckleberry Finn.* Alexander Graham Bell patents the telephone.

1877 Spontaneous railroad strikes across the nation presage the industrial warfare that was to flare up in the later 19th and early 20th centuries.

1883 Thomas A. Edison builds the first central electric power station, the Pearl Street Station in New York City. Congress closes off Chinese immigration for a decade and takes the first federal steps to restrict immigration from Europe.

1883 The Pendleton Act prescribes the start of the merit system in the federal civil service. Congress authorizes the first expenditures for rebuilding the low-ranking United States Navy into a seagoing force "second to none".

1886 The AFL, to be the bellwether of unionized labor for fifty years, is organized under the leadership of Samuel Gompers.

1887 The adoption of the Interstate Commerce Act marks the federal government's first venture into the regulation of big business.

1890 The Sherman Antitrust Act extends federal regulation of big business to manufacturing.

1892 The People's party is organized to carry the farmers' protest into national politics and nominates General James B. Weaver for president.

So, who is at fault? Is it you? Is it me? Is it them?

I take some of the blame for not paying attention to what the policy makers and lawmakers were doing under my very nose. I take the blame for pursuing the "American Dream" and blindly ignoring the traps and hurdles that are deceptively placed before me at every turn.

You too are at fault. For doing the same things that I did and for NOT doing anything at all. You say you didn't vote because your vote doesn't count. You only vote democrat. You only vote republican. You only vote for independents. You are only concerned with your community. You don't care what "they" do as long as it doesn't adversely affect you.

"They" are at fault for not being truthful and keeping the constitution in the forefront. They are at fault for not upholding the true meaning and discipline of the office in which they hold. They are at fault for succumbing to the greed and class division in which the dastardly deeds of their conduct are continuing to invoke.

If it sounds like I'm a little upset with the government, it's because I am. But I'm no fool. I know that there are proper and legal ways to deal with the government as well as voice your opinion. And this book is one of them.

I guess you could say it started when I was forced to sign up for the selective service (the military draft).

Well, I have to tell you a little story for it to hit home.

You see, I grew up in a small country town. We enjoyed a simple life with big dreams. I went to school and did what most small town kids did. I dreamed of someday leaving the country for the big city and seeing the world. Well, somewhere along the way about the 7th or 8th grade, we had a teacher ask us to write down what we wanted to be when we grew up. I wrote down a few things that I thought would be pretty cool to do. Looking back, they were probably things that I unconsciously had been exposed to or read about, or seen on television, or simply implanted. I wrote down three jobs or careers that I was thinking about at that time. They were to become a truck driver, to join the military, and to become an electrician. I can honestly say that I attempted all and achieved 2 of the 3. Out of the three, guess which one I did not achieve. It was joining the military.

I have had a successful career as an electronic technician and an industrial electrician. And for the last 15 years or so I have been enjoying a successful career in Information Technology. The elusive goal, however, was joining the military. It seems that the military, at that time, had a certain quota of denials that must be met, and I fell into that group, however slightly. Needless to say, I went onto college with other goals in mind. But here's the catch; once in college I was required, down right forced, to sign up for the selective service or else I would not receive any government loans. Now isn't that a blimp? I refused and was threatened with being dismissed from school. I even thoroughly explained that the government already knows all about me and I would not be able to serve. Even when I was willing and trying to serve! So I by no means was going to allow them to force me to sign this document against my will. Needless to say, this really did not sit well with me. But, as you can guess, who won that battle? For me,

I knew that my education was far more important, so I reluctantly signed up for the draft.

Smoke and mirrors. Smoke and mirrors.

It was at this point that I realized that the government was totally controlling its citizens with brutal force in an intricate and perceptive fashion. They knew how to get what they wanted from you and you would thank them for it. (*At that time it was the student loans at a rate of 8%. Again, I was at that time just an average American, not wealthy enough to pay for my education out of pocket.*)

Again I ask who is at fault. Is it the government? Is it the people who govern? Or is it an unseen force that affects us all and reminds us that we really have no control.

This is a rhetorical question; finding fault is not really important. However, finding solutions and a better way to uphold and implement the supreme law of this land is the real goal. So give it some thought and let's start discussing real solutions, strategies, and ways to implement change, change that goes beyond class, color, creed, and borders.

4

How Do We Escape?

So, how do we fix the problem? How do we make our voices heard, that enough is enough. What can we do to let the politicians and the big government know that the time has come for reckoning? You must answer for your dastardly deeds. We are sick and tired of being raped and pillaged by your immoral and unscrupulous ways. We want real change that will make our lives and those of our neighbors better.

How? We can fix problems by the very right that the supreme law of the land provides us. As the preamble starts out, "WE THE PEOPLE, in order to form a more perfect union," we the people must act. We must take action and take part in the political process from the very lowest level of government all the way up to the highest.

Many songwriters and artists have provided catchy and rhythmic tunes and accolades to fighting for your rights, for instance, Bob Marley wrote in his song, "Get Up Stand Up, stand up for rights; Don't give up the fight." It's time to take heed and be encouraged by those words and thoughts that were so elegantly pieced together that they still resonate in our hearts. Life is worth more and there is more to life than death and taxes.

Government does have a place in the world and even in our lives. However, that place and that reach should be limited. The founders of this country did not intend our government to have this much control over its citizens' lives. Government is supposed to focus on the well-being of its citizens and the protection of their liberties.

There are a lot of things that the government SHOULD DO and a lot of things that the government SHOULD NOT DO. One of the things that they should do is regulate some of these rogue agencies, companies, and organizations like the insurance companies, banks, health care, and mortgage companies. However, the government SHOULD NOT turn around and then give OUR tax dollars to a Bank, which will remain nameless here, and then tell them who they can or cannot lend money to or do business with.

HTS (Hypo-Thoughtful-Situation) ™

Let's say you are running a business making widgets and gadgets. Your employees are doing their jobs and getting a decent salary for doing what they are supposed to do. Then, there is one particular employee who is not doing what he is supposed to be doing and is wreaking havoc on everyone else. He is always late, leaves early, and is actually costing you more than just a salary. What do you do?

(I will not answer this for you. Here are a few lines where you may write your own answer.)

_____

_____

What do you do when a machine or a piece of equipment fails to operate as it is supposed to do? What do you do when something is broken and no longer provides you with the service which it was supposed to deliver?

When something is broken, you either fix it or you replace it. There is nothing difficult about that concept. You may have to order new parts to fix it. Some of those parts can be very expensive. So this leads to weighing your options of repair versus replacement. What do you do? Can you make it last much longer? How long will it last before it just completely shuts down or locks up and either leaves you stranded or costs you much more than the new part or entire replacement ever would?

What do you do?

The problem comes in when you TALK and TALK about how to fix it or how to replace it and what to replace it with. You talk and talk and never do anything. You begin to research, check around and even invite in 'salespeople' to see what's available, yet you never take action and nothing ever gets done.

We really need to think about what the government is doing to us. They are all for the most part, wealthy. So they don't ever really care about what the economy is doing as long as it does not affect THEIR lifestyle. They are constantly referring to 'us' as "The People", "The Taxpayers", "The Common Man", "The American Family", "The Average Joe", "The American People", "Somebody", "Every Man, Woman, and Child in this Country", and the newly created, "Joe the Plumber". What do all of these references have in common? All of these terms are in the third person sense. The politicians very rarely, if ever, include themselves in this context.

The pimp and his organization have truly proven over the last 9 months that they are in a completely different world that is peering down on "us". They are all over this land making rules and regulations, laws, and restrictions that affect our lives and livelihood. It does not affect them, only us. And this is a big problem. We have got to change this.

The US Senate

Do you think that the salaries of the members of Congress are too high? This topic has been a source of taxpayer unhappiness for years. The following link will provide some insight into the salaries of all the rank-and-file members of Congress.

http://usgovinfo.about.com/library/weekly/aa031200a.htm

Congress: Rank-and-File Members' Salary

The current salary (2009) for rank-and-file members of the House and Senate is $174,000 per year.

- Members are free to turn down pay increase and some choose to do so.

- In a complex system of calculations, administered by the Office of Personnel Management, congressional pay rates also affect the salaries of federal judges and other senior government executives.

- During the Constitutional Convention, Benjamin Franklin considered proposing that elected government officials not be paid for their service. Other Founding Fathers, however, decided otherwise.

Did you know that after serving only two years, a congressman or congresswoman gets lifetime benefits too?

As I'm writing this, they have passed a so-called economic stimulus package that is supposed to help stop the economic tail spin, and get our economy back on track. Ha! Then they start in with those third person innuendos again. They marvel about how it is supposed to do this and do that. Yet, I bet, not one senator, congressman, or representative, has thoroughly read through and completely comprehended what is contained within this so-called economic stimulus plan.

Yet, "we the people" continue to lose our jobs, our homes, and our means of living. Our friends, family, and loved ones are losing their lives in foreign and domestic wars. People are being "down-sized" and the small businesses and big companies alike are making the tough decisions and cutting back.

Just ask a wounded soldier, say one year after his/her injury, how the government is treating him/her and their family. This is another story

and I will not go into that here. But to our brave men and women and their families, we want to say this, "We the People" know that it is not your fault. WE support you and know that in that part of the pimp's organization you are contractually obligated to do what you are told – and if you rebel, the consequences are far greater than that of most civilians. Your contract basically strips you of all human rights and you then become a piece of government property to be used as they see fit.

I'm sorry, but I got sidetracked there for a moment. Now let's get back to the subject at hand.

Why is it so difficult for the government to create laws and do things that seem to be so plain and simple to us, "the everyday working man"? Why? Because THEY have completely LOST TOUCH

WITH REALITY. They really have NO CLUE anymore, what it is like trying to actually work and raise a family as a common peasant. As I have stated before, when you are wealthy you mentally live in a different world, and a lot of times the same rules and regulations DO NOT apply to you.

Now please do not get me wrong here, I'm not talking about wealth envy. I'm talking about politicians who are TAKING our tax dollars and doing what they please with them and lining their pockets and their estates through political favors and other 'legal' ways.

In regards to wealth envy, DON'T fall prey to it. Simply do not folks. Instead, let's join them. Let's join the wealthy, not the politicians. That's right, stop spending every penny, nickel and dime you get your hands on and buying STUFF that you don't really need or cannot afford; let us work toward joining the wealthy.

I certainly applaud the entrepreneurs that came up with an idea and started a business. You then worked your tail off and grew that business into a successful and profitable organization that can now sustain you and your family. As a matter of fact, you are helping others sustain their families as well. I applaud all of you that have toiled, struggled, sacrificed and taken risks to succeed and eventually made fortunes. I applaud those of you who have inherited your wealth and have done great things for your family and others for generations to come.

An Interesting Email

I received an email on 19 February 2009, entitled "Cut Backs". I found it rather amusing and thought I must share this with you. (Now keep in mind that this was circulating via email and you may have seen this already. I do not endorse or submit to the validity of the information contained herein. This is provided solely for entertainment. You may make your own decisions about the truth and validity of this and research the facts for yourself.)

BEGIN EMAIL

****

Subject: This will never happen

"The Proposal"

When a company falls on difficult times, one of the things that seems to happen is that they reduce their staff and workers. The remaining workers must find ways to continue to do a good job or take the risk that their job would be eliminated as well.

Wall Street and the media normally congratulate the CEO for making this type of "tough decision," and his board of directors gives him a big bonus.

Our government should not be immune from similar risks.

Therefore:

Reduce the strength of the House of Representatives from the current 435 members to 218.

Reduce Senate members from 100 to 50 (one per State). Then, reduce their staff by 25%.

Accomplish this over the next 8 years.

(Two steps/two elections) and of course this would require some redistricting.

Some Yearly Monetary Gains Include:

$44,108,400 through reduction in base pay for Congress. (267 members X $165,200 pay/member/ yr.)

$97,175,000 from elimination of their staff. (Estimate $1.3 Million for staff per each member of the House, and $3 Million for staff per each member of the Senate every year).

$240,294 from the reduction in the strength of the remaining staff by 25%.

$7,500,000,000 reduction in pork barrel earmarks each year. (Those members whose jobs are gone. Current estimates for total government pork earmarks are at $15 Billion/yr).

The remaining representatives would need to work smarter and improve efficiencies. It might even be in their best interests to work together for the good of our country!

We may also expect that smaller committees might lead to a more efficient resolution of issues as well. It might even be easier to keep track of what your representative is doing.

Congress has more tools available to do their jobs than it had back in 1911 when the current number of representatives was established. (Telephone, computers, cell phones, to name a few.)

Note: Congress did not hesitate to head home when it was a holiday, even when the nation needed a real fix to the economic problems. Also, we have 3 senators who have not been doing their jobs for the past 18+ months (on the campaign trail) and still they all have been accepting full pay. These facts alone support a reduction in the numbers of the members of the Senate and the House.

Summary of opportunity:

$ 44,108,400 through reduction of congress members.

$282,100, 000 from the reduced house member staff.

$150,000,000 from the elimination of senate member staff.

$59,675,000 through 25% reduction of staff for remaining house members.

$37,500,000 through 25% reduction of staff for remaining senate members.

$7,500,000,000 from reduction in pork added to bills by the reduction of congress members.

$8,073,383,400 per year is the estimated total savings. (That's 8-BILLION just to start!)

Big business does these types of cuts all the time.

If Congress were required to serve 20, 25 or 30 years (like everyone else) in order to collect retirement benefits, taxpayers could save a bundle.

Now they get full retirement benefits after serving only ONE term.

IF you are happy with how Congress spends our taxes, delete this message. Otherwise, I assume you know what to do.

****

END OF EMAIL

Do you think that email is amusing? Just imagine what a difference it would make if congress would step up to "help us" out by taking a pay-cut.

WAKE UP! WAKE UP! WAKE UP!

People, we need to wake up and pay attention to what the government is really doing. We need to get involved and get educated on OUR politics. READ. Learn how government is supposed to operate and what THEY are supposed to be doing. This is the only way we can initiate changes. This will be the only change that we can believe in. Change that YOU and I, "WE THE PEOPLE," eagerly await and strive for. We are taking part in our governance. We will hold those that we elect to these offices accountable. This is a must.

We must educate our children early on about politics and government and how to be productive and informed citizens. Don't stand by and allow your life and destiny to be controlled by someone who does not know you and your potential.

Parents, we must not allow children to drop out of school and continue to feed the system that pollutes our society with under educated, uneducated, and ill-informed youth with no direction or purpose in life.

We must hold each and every politician accountable for the job for which they were elected. We must hold them responsible for doing that which they took an oath to do to the best of their abilities and with the people's best interest in the forefront. When politicians are not held accountable and responsible, then we are at fault. We have allowed them this carte blanche lifestyle with no checks or consequences on poor management, misdeeds, or downright illegal actions that WE THE PEOPLE would otherwise pay a hefty price for.

We must all take an active part in being the checks and balances for a Pimp that is out of control. It's time for us to take some defensive stances against the 'in your face' politics.

In order to escape, we must wake up and not only take action against the politicians who blunder and fumble laws and regulations that directly affect our lives and livelihoods but also hold accountable businesses and employers that do business with and for the government, that waste YOUR and MY tax dollars needlessly. These companies charge extremely high rates and fees which they know the government will pay. These types of companies and the government know that they must continue to "pat each other's back," in order to keep padding their wallets at OUR (the taxpayers) expense.

There are some companies that charge reasonable and fair rates. And a lot of these companies are needed to do work for the government and the general public, mainly because the government simply cannot get the job done because of red tape and the lack of skills and knowledge. The problem comes about when greed and poor economics sneak into the picture. Well, sometimes it sneaks in. Most of the time greed is already built into these government contracts and jobs.

We must stop the greed and poor economic practices that have been driving us into the ground.

It is like we are on the "yellow brick road" seeking out the wizard. In fact, some of us get lost along this path seeking out the wizard and run off into the field and never return to the road. These are the hopeless ones that will never know just how much they're being pimped by the government. Nevertheless, some are true hearted and determined to find "the American Dream" by seeking out the great wizard to have all of their questions answered and find the truth. But once the wizard is found, all there is to see is 'smoke and mirrors' and with loud and continuous propaganda "Pay no Attention to the People behind the Curtain!"

Wake up! Wake up! Wake up! Look beyond the smoke and mirrors.

Although it might seem incredible at first, you must realize that they keep us dumb downed with 'tragic' national events that will grab our attention for months while they work their 'magic' behind the curtain. (Smoke and Mirrors!!)

If you were to take a look back, over the last 15 to 20 years, at any political platform, you will see that they promise the same things over and over. Health Care and taxes are the two most common topics for most political candidates from the local to the national level. They will also talk about education. Oh yes, they talk a very good deal and that's about all they do. No one has ever come up with a viable and reasonable solution for either of the issues. They talk about it and remark that something needs to be done, and most people will jump on that politician's bandwagon simply because he or she is talking about what they want to hear. They may even say that they will do something about it, but once they're elected, it is very little fan fare. Very little is done and then a few years later, there they go again with the same issues.

It's like the income tax. Every single politician in this country knows that the tax system is outdated, unfair, extremely complicated and almost impossible to make any sense of. Yet, they cannot and will not fix it. It's like I said in the beginning: it's broken, so either you fix it or you scrap it and get something new.

Our tax system is like that old jalopy that was purchased ages ago but which we will not get rid of it because it works. Doesn't matter how much it costs us to keep it working or how badly it pollutes the environment. The same is the case with the political system. They (the politicians) don't really care, because it really doesn't affect them. They don't have to ride in it or pay the bill for the maintenance and upkeep. We the people do. This one little system, taxes, causes the American people more stress, heartache, trouble, and downright ill will toward government than any other thing the government is responsible for. And to be fair, again, I remind you, I'm not talking about ALL politicians. Some of the folks we elect honestly and genuinely try very hard to work for the people.

I saw a bumper sticker recently on a passing vehicle. It simply stated: "Stop Bitching Start A Revolution". So out of curiosity I googled it; and let's just say that some of the links are very interesting. Some links give valid ideas and a few comments seem pretty good. One of them said it means just what it says; to stop talking about the problems and get involved with the political process. Well what exactly is that? Just what I'm trying to say in this book. WAKE UP! WAKE UP! WAKE UP!

With that, let's talk more about this Little Pimp called the IRS next, which is basically the Big Pimp's enforcer.

5

Three Little Big Words

Internal Revenue Service

The Little Pimp.

The **INTERNAL REVENUE SERVICE**. The name itself sets in your mind that WE, the government, will take your money and do with it what we please.

So what is the Internal Revenue Service? Why is it needed?

The Internal Revenue Service (IRS) is the United States federal government agency that collects taxes and enforces the internal revenue laws.

This Little Pimp is the enforcer of the Big Pimp's tax system that no one person completely understands. The system is so convoluted and complex that people must devote careers to understand it. Or should I say, trying to understand it. And the Pimps don't really want us to understand it, which is why they constantly make changes. The changes are made to keep them and their assets protected while all along they continue to rape and pillage the taxpayers, the working class Americans. The politicians and governmental pawns certainly don't get concerned about their taxes, because as I said they are in a different world. They all feel as if they are above the law and above the very rules and regulations that they themselves create.

Take a look back at history and see how it got started.

Bureau of Internal Revenue

In July 1862, during the Civil War, President Lincoln and Congress created the office of the Commissioner of Internal Revenue and enforced an income tax to pay war expenses (See the Revenue Act of 1862 for more information and details.). The position of the Commissioner exists today as the head of the Internal Revenue Service.

This organization was created to enforce the collection of these taxes and named so after the internal revenue to be collected (and was formerly called the "Bureau of Internal Revenue"), in contrast to U.S. government institutions that collected external revenue through duties and tariffs.

Now I ask you, is this Little Pimp still doing what it was initially tasked to do? I would venture to say yes and much, much more.

Why is the Internal Revenue Service needed when the Federal Government collects most of its income taxes through something called withholding, sales tax, property tax, and all sort of taxes that you don't even know about.

There are a ton of arguments about the legality of the Internal Revenue Service and about the requirement of filing a tax return. This argument is basically about the 16 amendments and their ratification. Was it properly ratified by all states? If it was not properly ratified, then this organization exists in violation of the 5th amendment. Here is the reason why I want you to read the constitution and see just what our government is supposed to be doing.

The government and this Little Pimp has been operating secretly and under cover for so long, doing whatever they want to, so that most of us have become accustomed to the humdrum routine of working for a living and paying whatever taxes "they" say we are "supposed" to pay.

I beg you to please read the constitution and try to understand what it is that the government is supposed to be doing for the people for whom they govern. We must wake up and pay attention. Start questioning why. Read the form W-4 that your employer is required to have you completed so that federal taxes can be taken from the income that you earn. The formW-4 states its purpose in the very first paragraph. Form W-4 is completed so that your employer can deduct the correct amount of taxes from your pay. So why do we need the IRS? Smoke and mirrors, smoke and mirrors.

Hypo-Thoughtful-Situation ™

What if we had to pay our taxes once a year, say on April 15th for the amount that the government says we should pay them based on what our employer states is our income? Every employee gets all the income for which they work the hours, throughout the year. Then we must sit down once a year and write the government checks for providing its services. Do you think you could do it? How much do you think it would really be?

I mean we pay no taxes on nothing we purchase but once a year. Add it all up, groceries, gas, everything. First of all, this would be tough on us, so thank goodness we don't have to do this. Yet the government handles it. However, this still does not explain the use and need of the IRS. Again, what purpose do they serve?

To show you how the power of this Little Pimp has been exploited, check out this statement made before the Senate Committee on Finance by Robert Edwin Davis of Dallas, Texas, on April 28, 1998. Mr. Davis is an attorney. His statements were made to the Senate Committee on Finance and are proof of how out of control they have become. See the statement for yourself at: http://finance.senate.gov/davis.htm

Also check out these links and see if the Internal Revenue Service makes sense to you.

Taxation in the US

This link will take you to Wikipedia and give you information on taxation in the United States. It explains that taxation in the US is a complex system that can include payment to at least four different levels of government as well as several other methods of taxation.

http://en.wikipedia.org/wiki/Taxation_in_the_United_States

Why we pay so much in taxes?

This link will give you information on just how much we actually pay in taxes in the United States. See for yourself just how much of your hard earned income actually goes to the government in the form of taxes.

http://nowandfutures.com/taxes.html

Historic tax rates.

This link will take you to a tax accounting firm's web site that provides information and education on taxes. This particular link gives information on the history of tax rates within the U.S.

http://hkmscpa.com/hist%20tax%20rates.htm

Question, have you ever been audited? How do you feel being audited by the Little Pimp?

Just look at what the Obama administration has gotten away with. Look at all of the nominees that have had Tax issues and other "concerns" that were raised and had to TURN DOWN a position. BUT, did any of them lose their current jobs? No, they did not. It's business as usual, now that the spotlight has been turned off and they have slithered back into the coffer of darkness to continue on with their shady deeds.

Look at the current head of this Little Pimp, called the IRS. Allegedly this person refused to pay taxes for 3 or more years though he obviously owed it. He never paid until he was "nominated" to lead this very organization! Learn also that he paid it the day before he knew he would be nominated! And still got the job! This is just one example of how some government officials get away with "murder," which the little guy goes to jail for. The current tax system is simply wrong and needs to be replaced. The only way in which we will ever see change is to get rid of what is currently in place. Then we will be forced to come up with a new solution.

Oh sure, you could yell, scream, and shout that this is an outrage! You can say just about anything you want, but in the end, THEY have the final say about one of THEIR own. And THEY HAVE THE RIGHTS! It's written in the law! That THEY wrote! WAKE UP PEOPLE!

It's time for every man, woman, and able-bodied child to start to take notice and take action. Educate yourself. Know what policies and governmental practices these politicians shove in our faces. They do it so blatantly and have done it for so long and so sneakily that we don't even see it. Can you say Smoke and Mirrors? Can you say the hand is quicker than the eye? The strange thing is that you see it and still don't believe it, yet you can do nothing about it.

That's right. They have brain washed us so that although we know what they are doing is so wrong, yet we do nothing but yell at the television, radio, or newspaper. In fact you certainly will not get within striking distance of the ones that really matter. And if you do, that other arm of the government called Law Enforcement will be on you so quickly that you'll think you've been "beamed" into an Ultimate Fight Challenge.

If you don't believe the Little Pimp has the power to wreck your world, just ask some of these people.

S. Jackson and J. Turner, former IRS agents, state that they themselves cannot find a law that requires Americans to pay Federal Income Tax. There is no law or statute in the constitution that requires you to file a federal income tax return.

Check out www.paynoincometax.com where Irwin Schiff makes challenges to the IRS and to tax accountants.

Here are a few other things you can read and judge for yourself. While reading these things, keep the U.S. Constitution in the forefront of your mind.

Also see the video on YouTube, Federal Income Tax – Why You Should Not Pay....very interesting.

Check out USAToday July 7, 2000, about the 16th amendment.

Grace Commission report 1984, Ronald Reagan . . .

What is the difference between conspiracy and strategy?

I must state at this point again that this book is to get you to think and educate yourself on those that govern you. I challenge you to prove anything written herein as fact or fiction, on whether the government is a pimp. Can we, as ordinary citizens, honestly and truly ever know exactly how much we pay in taxes? Can we as working class taxpayers ever really know our true income without tax?

Well, let's see if we can actually see just how much we really pay in the next chapter.

6

What Are We Really Paying?

Taxes, Taxes, Taxes

Income Taxes, Payroll Taxes, State Taxes, Federal Taxes, Sales Taxes, Property Taxes, Vehicle Taxes, Hidden Taxes, Unseen Taxes, Death Taxes.

We pay a lot of taxes and there appears to be no end in sight. There are actually more new taxes on the horizon that most of us have heard about. And for the most part there is not a lot that you can do to stop them from coming.

What taxes are we really paying? How many taxes do we really pay?

Let's do an exercise. Get one of your last check stubs. That is if you're working and paying taxes. Now if you're one of those "under the radar" cats reading this book, then this chapter is not for you. Heck, this book isn't for you. You can take a break here and go hustle some more cash for your private stockpile. But if you ARE one of those and you've gotten this far, I'd suggest that you keep on reading. You just might learn something.

What's that? You don't have a stockpile. You silly rabbit. Then what the heck are you doing with your cash? If you're not stashing it away for your own retirement, you should. Either way, you should stick around and read this chapter so you can see why I really chose to write this book. How this Little Pimp is actually worse than the big Pimp.

Take a look at how much the Little Pimp collected for the big Pimp.

This link will show a chart of how much federal tax was collected by each state for the year 2007.

http://en.wikipedia.org/wiki/Federal_tax_revenue_by_state

These totals represent the gross federal tax revenue collected by the IRS from each U.S. state, the District of Columbia, and Puerto Rico for 2007.

Gross collections	Population	Revenue/captia
$2,674,007,818,000	305,562,616	$8,528.22 (US Avg.)

Need help? That's over 2 Trillion Dollars. That's right, trillion with a CAPITAL T.

Can you say FAT CAT! (Yeah, yeah I know, this picture looks nothing like a cat, but you get the point.)

Here are the figures from the official site of the IRS at www.irs.gov.

Fiscal Year	2008
Corporate Income tax	$354,315,825
Individual Income tax	$1,425,990,183
Employment taxes	$883,197,626
Estates taxes	$26,543,433
Gift tax	$3,280,502
Excise tax	$51,707,840
Total	$1,780,306,008
Total Internal Revenue Collections	**$2,745,035,410**

Let's talk very briefly about some of these taxes that you pay, but you probably have no clue what they are for.

FICA Tax. What the heck is FICA?

Federal Insurance Contributions Act tax

The Federal Insurance Contributions Act (FICA) tax (pronounced fika) is a United States payroll (or employment) tax imposed by the federal government on both employees and employers to fund Social Security and Medicare—federal programs that provide benefits for retirees, the disabled, and children of deceased workers. Social Security benefits include old-age, survivors, and disability insurance (OASDI); Medicare provides hospital insurance benefits. The amount that one pays in payroll taxes throughout one's working career is directly tied to the social security benefits annuity that one receives as a retiree. This has led some to claim that the payroll tax is not a tax because its collection is directly tied to a benefit.

Social Security Tax

Not that most of us will ever see any of this money, but we still have to pay it.

Social Security is a social insurance program funded through dedicated payroll taxes called Federal Insurance Contributions Act (FICA). Tax deposits are formally entrusted to Federal Old-Age and Survivors Insurance Trust Fund, or Federal Disability Insurance Trust Fund, Federal Hospital Insurance Trust Fund or the Federal Supplementary Medical Insurance Trust Fund. The main part of the program is sometimes abbreviated as OASDI (Old Age, Survivors, and Disability Insurance) or RSDI (Retirement, Survivors, and Disability Insurance).

Talk about the past! You know who signed this into law, Franklin D. Roosevelt, as part of the New Deal.

Well, frankly my dear, I think it's time for another New Deal. Can the new administration deliver something better? I doubt it. Can they fix the outdated, convoluted, excessively cumbersome and complicated tax code we have today? Well, they could, but they won't. And will they not consider, because they will lose control? They will lose control of the amount of income they are able to collect through taxes.

Take a look at your paycheck stub. Look at your gross and then look at your net. What is the amount? Now how much of that is being paid in taxes? What is the percentage of that amount for taxes?

Perhaps you're paying your fair share with each paycheck for the year. I mean, the government is the one that started the 'withholding'. Are they not smart enough to figure out what we paid without us having this one-day a year that we must submit to the enforcer?

I'm pretty sure you have heard this little saying: "we work the first three months of the year to pay the government". Well, let us take a look at a real paycheck and see what takes away from your hard-earned pay. Let's take a look at why you work all night and weekends, and try to get all the overtime and extra shifts to make up the difference.

This is taken from an actual paycheck with the numbers obscured a bit to protect the innocent, or guilty, or whichever way you want to look at it.

SMALL COMPANY A

Company: Small Company A		Net Pay:	$1,608.00
Address: 1234 Main St		Pay Period Begin:	
Big City, USA		Pay Period End:	
		Check Date:	

Employee

Name:	MidClass Worker	SSN:	000-00-0000
Address:	000 My Street	Status:	
	My City, USA	Federal Allowance: 4	

Tax Info

Fed Status:		State Status:	
Fed Allowances:	4	State Allowance:	4
Fed Addl %:		State Addl %:	
Fed Addl Amt:		State Addl Amt:	

Pay Summary	Current		YTD Amt
Salary	2,698.00		70,148.00
Total Tax	403.00		10,478.00
Total Deductions	670.00		17,420.00
Net Pay		1625.00	42,250.00
Before Tax Deductions			
	-453.00		11,778.00
	-46.00		1,196.00
	-7.00		182.00
	-139.00		3,614.00
Total		-645.00	16,770.00
After Tax Deductions			
	-9.00		234.00
	-8.00		208.00
	-8.00		208.00
	-25.00		650.00
Taxes			
Federal Withholding	-152.00		3,952.00
Federal MED/EE	-30.00		780.00
Federal OASDI/EE	-134.00		3,484.00
State Withholding	-87.00		2,262.00
Total	403.00		10,478.00

After reviewing the check stub, you can see that you actually do work the first three to four months of the year, just to meet your tax obligations to the big Pimp. Fascinating, is it not?

Now can someone tell me why is it then that the Pimp requires you to wade through paper work once a year and submit to them, how much money you made. Don't they know already? Wasn't that the reason you completed the Pimp's "W-4" form for your employer?

Is the pimp ignorant of all this? He knows how much a worker makes because he gets his cut up front! This pimp knows how much you make even before you get your first paycheck! They even know how much you've made during your working lifetime.

Have any of you received your statement of earnings from the Social Security Administration? This statement is an indication of the amount reported as income from all of your employers since you began completing that government form W-4.

Do you wonder why so many people work extra part-time jobs or do other work to try and get paid under the table or get paid in cash? The Pimp doesn't want you to make cash transactions, because they cannot track you when you use cash. So they have your employer get as much traceable and tractable information on you as humanly possible.

Your check stub has your federal identification number and all of your "zero-in-on-you" information. This way the big Pimp can seize your life at any given moment.

Other taxes we pay include sales tax on food, shelter, and clothing. Here is another example of how we pay taxes and fees to the government that is sometimes overboard. To protect the innocent, I will not name the state, but this is with regard to owning a vehicle in this state. As you know, there are numerous costs associated with owning a vehicle, and yes, a tax is one of them. So let's start at the beginning.

When you first purchase your shiny new vehicle, you pay the infamous fees to the government called Tax, Tag, and Title. If you break those three items down, you will see that the government is getting paid three times.

I have a little task for you. Visit the IRS website (www.irs.gov). See if you can locate the current tax code. See if the very organization that supposedly follows this code and enforces it upon taxpayers makes it easy and readily available to you to see it, read it, and understand it.

You would think that the IRS website is one which will enable you to educate yourself on what the tax code is and what it means. What are the do's and don'ts for the average working taxpayer? If you, as a working taxpayer, were supposed to adhere to the tax codes and laws of the governing entity that governs you, wouldn't you want to know what the rules are?

Go on, take a break here and see what you can find. Here are a few lines for you to take some notes.

_____

_____

_____

_____

Once you have made an attempt to search for the code, we will take a look at some ideas of "What If". For example, what if we just don't file that yearly paperwork? Well, as long as you don't "owe" the Pimp, they could care less if you file. But oh buddy, if you owe the Pimp and you don't file. As Mr. T from the A-Team says, "I pity the fool".

7

What If?

Take a look at history. You can see that even in the good old days people got fed up with paying extremely high and unnecessary taxes. Remember that little tea party thrown in Boston?

What if we did something like that today? What if every law abiding honest citizen, employer, entrepreneur, business, company, or organization, were to simply stop paying taxes? What do you think the actual repercussions would be?

They couldn't PIMP SLAP us ALL! But I'm pretty sure they would have one hell of a time trying.

How long do you think government would last? How long would our current way of living and surviving last? Would you do it? Could you do it?

Heck No! And don't even try it! PAY YOUR TAXES PEOPLE!

Don't even think of not paying and trying to hide. The Pimp and his organization is too good and have so many ways and means to find you, get you, and shake every nickel, dime, and quarter out of you.

What if you don't pay your State/Local taxes? There are some states that don't have a "STATE" tax. Or at least they tell you they don't. It's not on the books anyway. Mmm… boy oh boy, you better believe they make up for it in many other ways.

America is a great country, right? What makes it so great? If it's so great, then why do we have some of the problems that 'developing' countries have?

I mean we have hunger issues right here in America. We have homelessness, drug problems, unemployment problems, gang problems, and education problems, problems with people not getting proper medical care that is needed to save their lives. You can drive to just about any major US city and you will see these things and more. You can even go to some of the remote rural areas of this great land and still see poverty and in some cases even the "slave mentality" is still in existence.

Why? How could this be? Are we too big and too great! I don't think so.

So how could we, America, have these types of problems in our own backyard, yet continue to be a world leader. Why?

Because a lot of us are sleepwalking through this haze of smoke and mirrors on the yellow brick road looking for a pot of gold at the end of a rainbow.

WAKE UP! WAKE UP! WAKE UP!

Snap out of it! Look at what we are doing to ourselves, to our children, and to their children. We must pay attention to what is really going and stop being so wasteful.

I often ask people to imagine this . . .

Whoever you are, wherever you are, just think about your work, your current work or some work you did in the past. You are making a very good salary. Imagine that you had absolutely no debt whatsoever, other than your basic living expenses. I mean no debt at all. Your home is paid for, your autos are paid for, all of your "Stuff" is paid in full and you only have to pay your property taxes and income taxes.

Go ahead, take a few moments to think about it. This is your What If moment; go ahead, enjoy it.

That would be great, wouldn't it? You could do some of the things that you've always wanted to do. You could save more money for retirement. You could invest more for retirement. You could send your kids to that private school you've always dreamed of. You could start that business that has been burning in your mind. You could take a real vacation. You could spend more time with your family. You could do a number of things if you could only get out of the race with the other rats, if you could only get off that 'treadmill' (more like dreadmill) to nowhere.

Well, in order to do that my friends, you must, say with me . . .

WAKE UP! WAKE UP! WAKEUP!

Free your mind of the nonsense that is filling your lives every single day. Educate yourself on what it takes for YOU to survive and be happy -- not what society or the government, or the media, or anyone else says will make you happy and content. But you must find it.

The politicians don't really concern themselves with the average citizen's problems and issues, but there is one time every few years when they do exactly that and that is during election time. The rest of the time, they are busy pestering us with their rules and regulations that most of them don't even follow.

Here is a prime example to show how the Pimp and his organization are being elitist. They are in a different world and would rather die than give it up.

Here, as recently as in April 2009, a senator jumped from one political party to another, just to save his hide and remain in elitist power. He figured he was at the end of the line with his current party and decided to bail out before election time. I'm sure this is not new and it's been done before. But it just goes to show that he was thinking, 'if I lose, I'm out. I'm out of the club with all the perks and privileges. I might have to go back to being an "average citizen". I can't let my 25 plus years of public service go for nothing.' Sickening, downright sickening.

What if we had term limits? Yeah, that would do it.

You know Mr. Senator, out here in the real world, or should I say, down here in the real world, there is no more cradle-to-the-grave employment.

Oh, but wait! He's not one of us! He's in that Pimp's organization and they do take care of his or her own. Oh well, folks, it was fun, wasn't it? Seeing a politician squirm.

Anyway, I guess since we do have politicians who have been in public service for 20 or 30 plus years, they have truly seen what works and what doesn't. And they have learned what to do, how to do it, when to do it, and to whom to do it to. That experience keeps this great machine chuggin' right along. With all of its quirks, jerks, and loose parts, it's still leading the way whether on the road or off; we're still the leader of the pack.

8

Still Number One

The United States of America

Even with all of our problems and issues, this country is still a leader. People around the world still either love this country or hate this country. Number one to love, number one to hate. Yet we persist and prevail with valor, honor, dignity, and respect.

Think about it. If you went around the world and asked everyone you met, that if they had a free pass to go to any country in the world, which country they would rank at the number one spot? Go ahead, make a list. List the top 5.

1. _____

2. _____

3. _____

4. _____

5. _____

Whether you are rich or poor, America is probably the best country in the world to be.

If you are rich, you can have the best of the best at your finger tips. The Pimp sees you as a cash cow, mainly because you will create jobs for the poor and the middle-class to continue their revenue streams.

If you are poor, you can get help. All you have to do is ask. There are programs after programs, from the Pimp's organization, that are willing to help. But they don't make it easy for you. You almost have to be below the poverty level to get assistance. You are the piece of the puzzle that keeps the rich cash machines going for them.

So you see, it is a win-win for everyone. The lines are clearly drawn and everyone pretty much knows their place.

So when will you… ☺ …. Say it with me…

WAKE UP!

> **WAKE UP!**

> **WAKE UP!**

And realize that this is NOT a dream world. YOU can and DO make a difference. YOU can be more, YOU can achieve more, YOU can do more.

Start with doing what is possible, stay focused, remain flexible and adaptable, and before you know it, you will be accomplishing the impossible.

T H E   E N D

I want to thank you so much for purchasing my book. I hope it was really entertaining, inspiring and educational.

As our famous leader said, there are two things you can count on and that is, death and taxes. I say it should only be one, because the other is something that we should be able to control.

"When the people fear their government, there is tyranny; when the government fears the people, there is liberty." - Thomas Jefferson

APPENDIX

THE CABINET

Again, at the time I was writing this, a lot of administration changes were taking place. Most of the holders of the positions listed here may or may not be correct.

The tradition of the Cabinet dates back to the beginnings of the Presidency itself. Established in Article II, Section 2, of the Constitution, the Cabinet's role is to advise the President on any subject he may require advice about, relating to the duties of each member's respective office.

The Cabinet includes the Vice President and the heads of 15 executive departments — the Secretaries of Agriculture, Commerce, Defense, Education, Energy, Health and Human Services, Homeland Security, Housing and Urban Development, Interior, Labor, State, Transportation, Treasury, and Veterans Affairs, as well as the Attorney General.

In the order of succession to the Presidency:
Vice President of the United States
Joseph R. Biden

Department of State
Secretary: Hillary Rodham Clinton

Department of the Treasury
Secretary: Timothy F. Geithner

Department of Defense
Secretary: Robert M. Gates

Department of Justice
Attorney General: Eric H. Holder, Jr.

Department of the Interior
Secretary: Kenneth L. Salazar

Department of Agriculture
Secretary: Thomas J. Vilsack

Department of Commerce
Secretary: Gary F. Locke

Department of Labor
Secretary: Hilda L. Solis

Department of Health and Human Services
Secretary: Kathleen Sebelius

Department of Housing and Urban Development
Secretary: Shaun L.S. Donovan

Department of Transportation
Secretary: Raymond L. LaHood

Department of Energy
Secretary: Steven Chu

Department of Education
Secretary: Arne Duncan

Department of Veterans Affairs
Secretary: Eric K. Shinseki

Department of Homeland Security
Secretary: Janet A. Napolitano

Council of Economic Advisors
Chair: Christina Romer

Environmental Protection Agency
Administrator: Lisa P. Jackson

Office of Management & Budget
Director: Peter R. Orszag

United States Trade Representative
Ambassador: Ronald Kirk

United States in the United Nations
Ambassador: Susan Rice

Chief of Staff
Rahm I. Emanuel

WHITE HOUSE STAFF

Chief of Staff
Rahm Emanuel

Deputy Chiefs of Staff
Jim Messina
Mona Sutphen

Senior Advisors
David Axelrod
Valerie Jarrett
Pete Rouse

In addition, the following entities exist within the White House Office:

- Advance
- Appointments and Scheduling
- Office of the Cabinet Liaison
- Chief of Staff's Office
- Office of Communications
- Office of Energy and Climate Change Policy
- Office of the First Lady
- Homeland Security Council
- Office of Legislative Affairs
- Office of Management and Administration
- Oval Office Operations
- Office of Political Affairs
- Office of Presidential Personnel
- Office of Public Liaison and Intergovernmental Affairs
- Office of the Press Secretary
- Office of Social Innovation
- Office of the Staff Secretary
- Office of Urban Affairs Policy
- Office of the White House Counsel
- White House Fellows

The US Senate

Credit: U.S. Senate, 110th Congress, Senate Photo Studio

Do you know who your senator is and what he/she is supposed to do for you? If not, please, get busy and find out. Here is space for you to write the names of your current senators.

My Senators

_____

_____

What is Government and Why do we Need it?
http://www.anarchistnews.org/?q=node/671

What is government?
http://www.geocities.com/humanitiesproj/

An essay about the origin and evolution of government including an analysis of the history of government based upon the ideas of John Lock:
www.geocities.com/humanitiesproj/ -

What is government?
See the book *Principles of Sociology with Educational Applications*, by Frederick R. Clow.

The Executive Branch
http://www.whitehouse.gov/our_government/executive_branch/

The Legislative Branch
http://www.whitehouse.gov/our_government/legislative_branch/

The Judicial Branch
http://www.whitehouse.gov/our_government/judicial_branch/

Politics and Policy in States and Communities – John J. Harrington; Little, Brown and Company

The American Republic, Volume Two: since 1865 – Hosfstadter, Miller, and Aaron; Prentice-Hall

"no taxation without representation"

http://en.wikipedia.org/wiki/No_taxation_without_representation

http://en.wikipedia.org/wiki/Internal_Revenue_Service

House of Representatives: Members 435, including 6 DC, Puerto Rico and the five US Territories

The Senate: 100 (2 for each state)

Variables

17 Senate Committees

70 Sub Committees

23 House Committees

104 Subcommittees

The House and the Senate combined make up the Congress.

Things to research and people, organizations, and causes to contact and ask questions and get some insight.

The Heritage Foundation

Americans for Fair Taxation

Where do you fall in one of these "categories"?
Liberal
Socialist
Communist
Conservative
Democrat
Republican
Don't really care

About the Author

Bernard Copeland is your average American Citizen. He was born and raised in the small, but historic town of Warm Springs, Georgia, growing up as a typical small town kid playing sports and band in school. Then go off to college and obtained two Technical degrees. This book is his first published work, yet he hopes to write and publish many more works that will enlighten, entertain, and inspire you to do more and get more out of life.

ORDER FORM

ORDER FORM

Send Certified Funds to:

TGIAP c/o Bernard Copeland
P.O. Box 0736
Redan, GA 30074-0736

Please send me _____ books at $14.95 each plus $2.00 to cover the tax that the pimp requires I collect.

Name: _____

Address: _____

City: _____ State: _____ Zip: _____

Telephone: _____

Email address: _____

ORDER FORM

Send Certified Funds to:

TGIAP c/o Bernard Copeland
P.O. Box 0736
Redan, GA 30074-0736

Please send me _____ books at $14.95 each plus $2.00 to cover the tax that the pimp requires I collect.

Name: _____

Address: _____

City: _____ State: _____ Zip: _____

Telephone: _____

Email address: _____